CHALLENGING MAZES

48 New and Unusual Puzzles

BY

LEE DANIEL QUINN

DOVER PUBLICATIONS, INC., NEW YORK

Published in Canada by General Publishing
Company, Ltd., 30 Lesmill Road, Don Mills,
Toronto, Ontario.
Published in the United Kingdom by Constable
and Company, Ltd.

Challenging Mazes: 48 New and Unusual Puzzles
is a new work, first published by Dover Publications, Inc., New York, in 1975.

International Standard Book Number: 0-486-21177-0
Library of Congress Catalog Card Number: 75-2822

Manufactured in the United States of America
Dover Publications, Inc.
180 Varick Street
New York, N. Y. 10014

INTRODUCTION

For hundreds of years, people have enjoyed being perplexed by mazes, whether in the form of paths through heavy greenery (as at the Hampton Court palace near London) or labyrinths such as those alleged to be in the palace of Minos on Crete, or those dating from 2300 B.C. in ancient Egypt. Mazes on a flat surface, making an unusual design, can be found in the pavements of medieval churches and may have originated in the Catacombs of Rome.

The mazes in this book, offspring of those flat-surface mazes, are all of my own design, and are of two types. The first, from "Start Out" to "Boomerang," pp. 1–24, are fairly straightforward, follow-the-path mazes, though of varying difficulty. The second half, from "Fine Fourth" to "Brickyard," pp. 25–48, are much more unusual, perhaps unlike any mazes you've seen before. These have some special requirements or circumstances that make them unique. In both groups mazes are arranged in order of difficulty, beginning with fairly easy ones and ending with some that will offer considerable puzzlement even to the experienced maze-solver.

Solutions begin on page 49, but I suggest you consult them only after your own efforts have failed. Solutions represent, of course, the shortest possible path meeting the requirements of the puzzle. For each puzzle, unless otherwise specified, you're to start at the top and finish at the bottom.

A few mazes, such as the one on page 1, "Start Out," are solid, or "under and over," mazes. On puzzles of this type, when one path runs under another, you follow it around regardless of the lines crossing it.

Usually, though, a line across your path is the signal to turn back and try again. Each maze, however, carries its own instructions, and its own challenge.

LEE DANIEL QUINN

Old Bridge, New Jersey
February, 1975

To Sandmah
who has passed on to me
her unique way
of looking at things

1. START OUT

That's right! Start your outbound journey in the center. Make sure you pass no arrows going the wrong way. And — finish either at the top or bottom. OK? Now start out!

2. VASE & KEY

Here's a restful puzzle that should be a breeze. How about a 90-second time limit?
Start at the top, finish at the bottom.

3. LETTERMIX

These letters do not make up words, they're there to provide one clear path from top to bottom. Should be as simple as A-B-C!

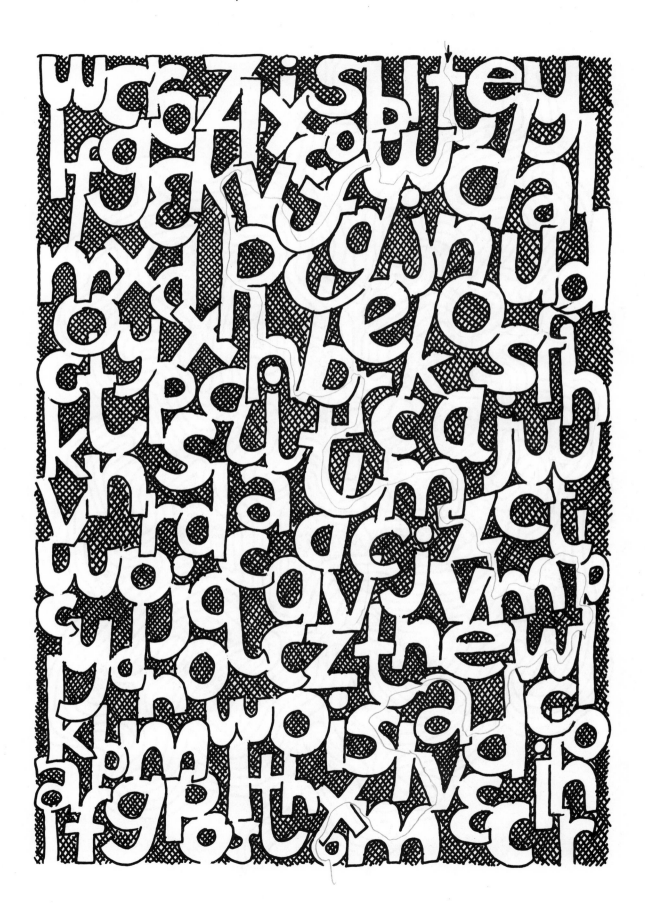

4. PARK RIDE

Imagine this to be the map of the roads around a number of parks. You may enjoy the bucolic splendor but, alas, must travel from top to bottom . . . obeying the one-way arrows, of course!

5. K-RATION

There's just a big enough ration of "Ks" to make one path from top to bottom. Don't worry if you see a few "Xs" and "Ys." They are there to make your journey more fun!

6. DERANGEMENT

You'll be a little deranged before you find the right path from top to bottom in this kinky pattern. Well, a little mad is better than none!

7. BONZAI

I can't claim this design. It's a traditional oriental pattern. My job was to change it from the "scrutable" to the "inscrutable"! How did I do?

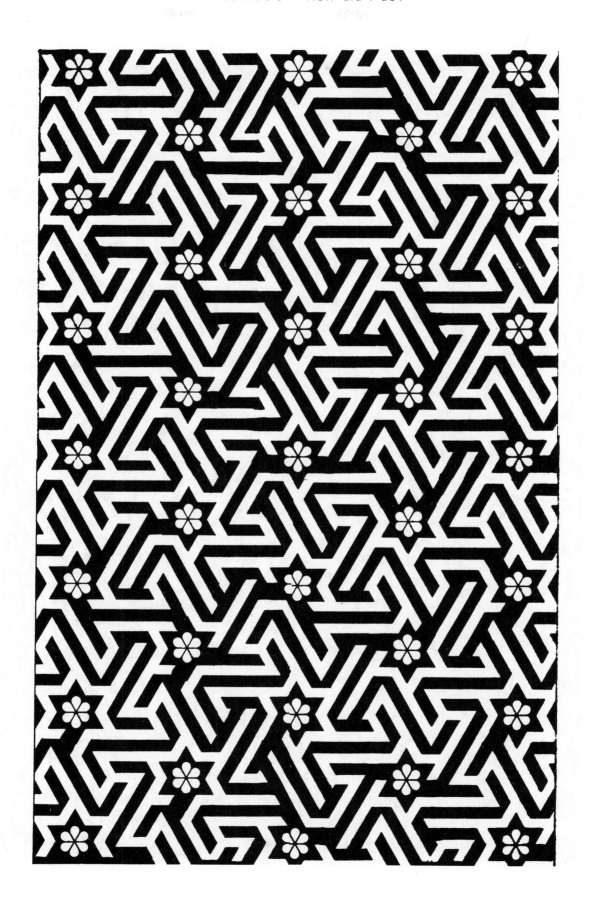

8. BUBBLE BOUNCE

These dancing bubbles will "pop your mind," if you let them. There is no soft-soap in finding the answer here! Just hard work!

9. TAILSPIN

Another classic circle design, with a few extra circles to make it more difficult. From top to bottom is your chore.

10. FLORAL DESIGN

Start at the top, flit through the flower, and come out at the bottom. Watch out for pollen if you have an allergy to work!

11. CRUMPLES

Among and between the edges of all this "crumpled paper" you'll find just one open path from top to bottom. This puzzle's a "shredder."

12. NEXI

Webster tells us that a nexus is a link or a means of communication. Its plural is nexus or nexuses, but these shapes look more like nexi to me; hence nexi is the title of this maze. There's only one way from top to bottom!

13. INTERMANGLE

The spelling of the title is intended. Somewhere in this mangled under-and-over intermingling of paths is the one that leads out at the bottom.

14. HE WENT THATAWAY

With so many arrows in this design, one of them must point the right path from top to bottom. While a pretty print, the puzzle's easy . . . just follow the arrows!

14. HE WENT THATAWAY

15. MASQUE

When this mask begins to smile at you, watch out! You're in trouble. One tip, the ''background'' may be part of the maze!

16. LADYBUGS

My daughter claims there are three ladybugs in the center of this maze. Your problem is, like all ladybugs, to fly away home.

17. ALLEY TRAP

Here's a puzzle to box your ears! While it would seem that going from top to bottom would have you go down all alleys, you'll soon find out differently.

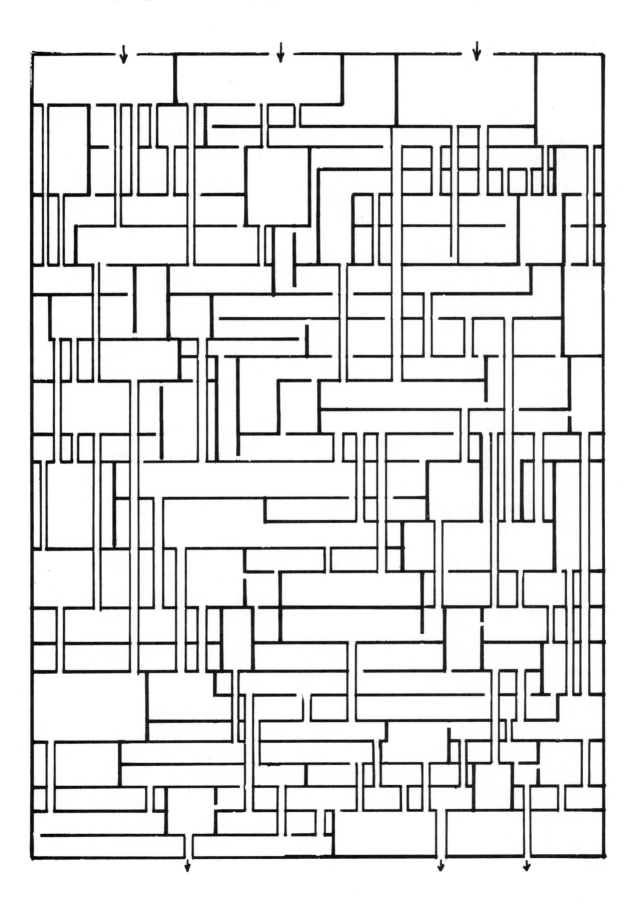

18. BLACK STOPS

The black spots are stops that turn you back. So, this puzzle is filled with black
spot back stops — a tongue twister if there ever was one. Top to bottom is the move.

18. BLACK STOPS

19. CUBE ROUTE

This pattern is made up of optical illusion cubes in a design that I have adapted to a maze. As usual, it's in at the top — out at the bottom.

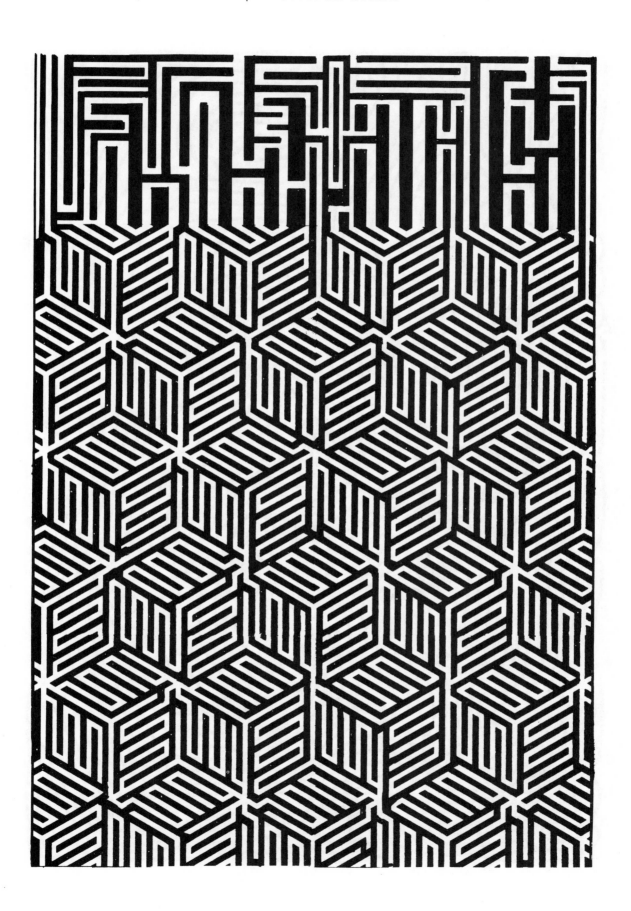

20. TEST PATTERN

The only "tests" this pattern gives you is to test your eyes and your patience. Notice how you keep seeing gray lines where the paths bend together.

21. QUILTIN' BEE

Here's a "crazy quilt" that may very well get you the same way. Be sure to take your Dramamine, you'll be going 'round and 'round so many times you'll need it!

22. HIGHWAY SIGNS

Here's a pattern of highway sign symbols repeated over and over. The paths weave in and out with only one emerging at the bottom. STOP at intersections and look for other paths.

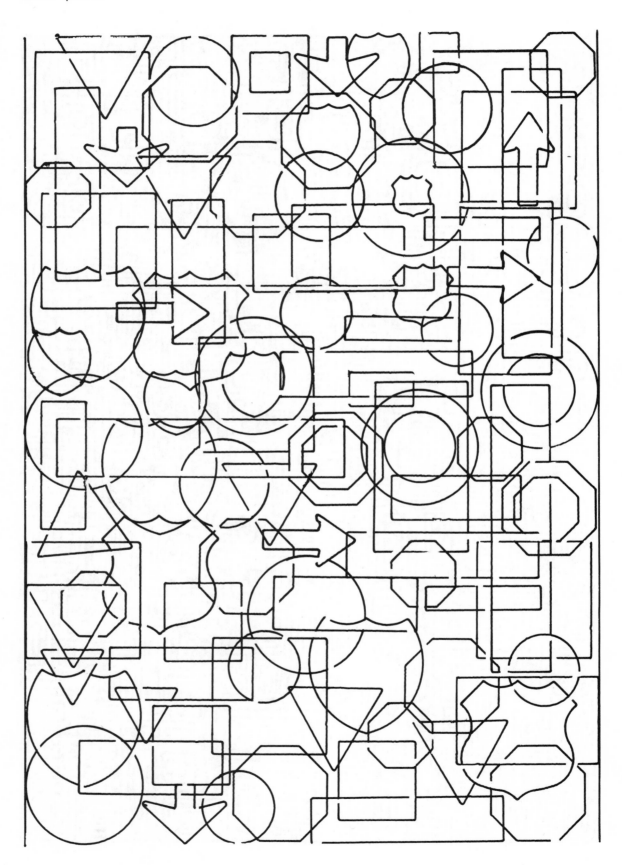

23. BORGIA'S COMPLAINT

The Borgias were very partial to poisoning their enemies. The worm turned when a smart rival thought up this maze to drive them mad.

23. BORGIA'S COMPLAINT

24. BOOMERANG

When you stop bouncing back and forth, one of these paths drops you out through the bottom. This is a real Dingo! (That's an Australian dog.)

25. FINE FOURTH

Here are a clutch of patriotic symbols that sit in the middle of some of the paths. Your job is to get out (through one of the two exploding firecrackers) WITHOUT going past any other symbols.

26. PINBALL

Start at either of the two arrows at the top and bounce from one "bumper" to another. Your object is to get a score of exactly 100 and then get out. You may not use any number more than once. No tilting please!

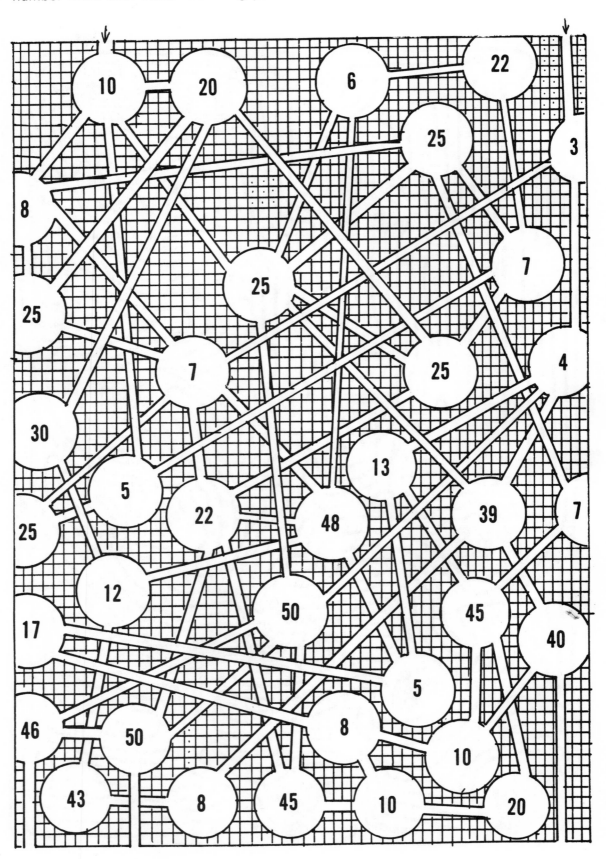

27. OUTBOUND

Here's one of those puzzles where you bust out. Starting from the center, there's only one path to the outside. North, south, east or west, only one is best!

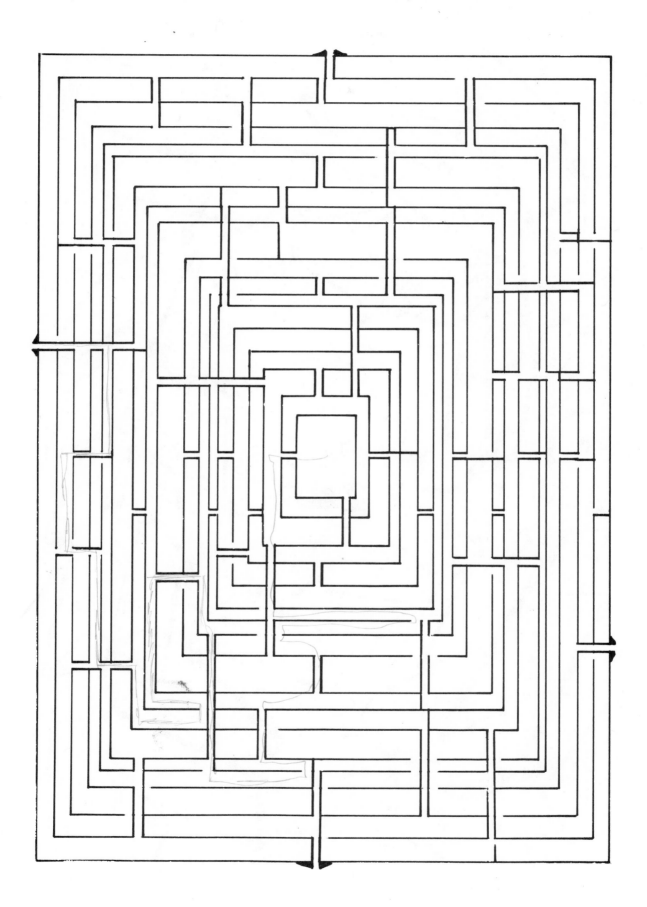

28. WILLIAM TELLS

Big Bill shot that apple off little Willey's head but I'm sure he didn't use the flight of arrows shown here. But, to get a nice cool drink at the center fountain, simply follow the opening in the arrows.

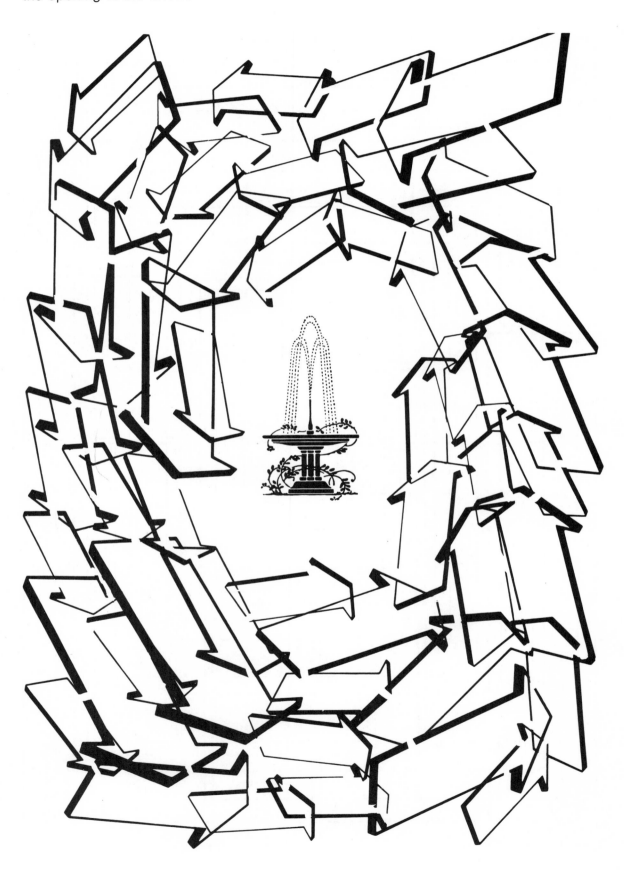

29. LETTER JUMP

Start at the top, choose a branching path and you'll come to a letter (say, E). You may then jump to a similar letter (another E, say), and follow that path to a different letter (say, B), etc. Finally, one path emerges at the bottom.

30. MONKEY SEE . . .

If this doesn't look like a monkey to you — that's OK. In any case, your job is to start at the top and get to the asterisk. Now — monkey do!

31. TANGLED WEB

"Oh! what a tangled web" the old saying starts. Well, this one will deceive you with all its over-and-under wanderings. Just find out which top letter ends with the same bottom letter.

32. NO! NO!

Almost all paths go through from top to bottom. However, there are four "no-no's" that may not be passed. Likewise, the "yes" areas are OK to pass through. Ready? Yes?

33. ANGLES & CURVES

A half-and-half problem to please the solvers who like curvy puzzles and the traditionalists who like squared-off mazes. You'll be going back and forth to find the way out.

34. EVEN MONEY

The odds are a lot greater than even money against your solving this one! Start at the top, collect an EVEN NUMBER of points and get out at the bottom. You can't use the same number twice!

35. BOLD LINES

Call 'em dots or spots — they're not nice! Here seems to be an easy pattern to go through from top to bottom . . . if it wasn't for the dots. To make it easy for you(!), you are allowed to gather one dot on your journey — two dots and you're out. Dot's right!

36. MIXMAZE

Here's a combination of under-and-over plus standard maze and then back to under-and-over again! The right "mix" whips up a quick solution.

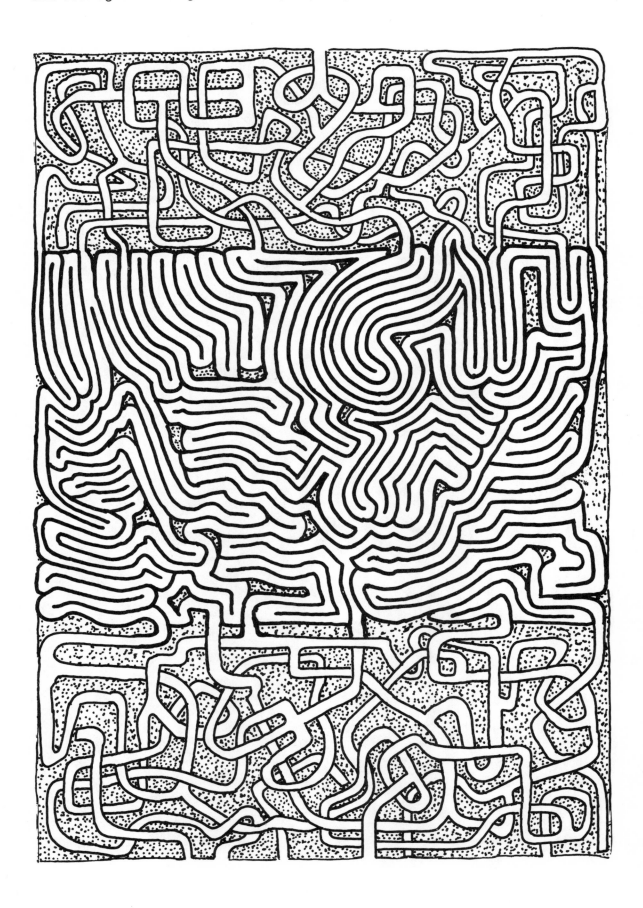

37. ETAOIN SHRDLU

To a typesetter these two strange words mean to ignore the previous material as it is going to be reset. He got this letter combination by running his finger along a line of keys on his typesetter. Anyway, go along a path in alphabetical order (not every letter is used) to find your way from top to bottom.

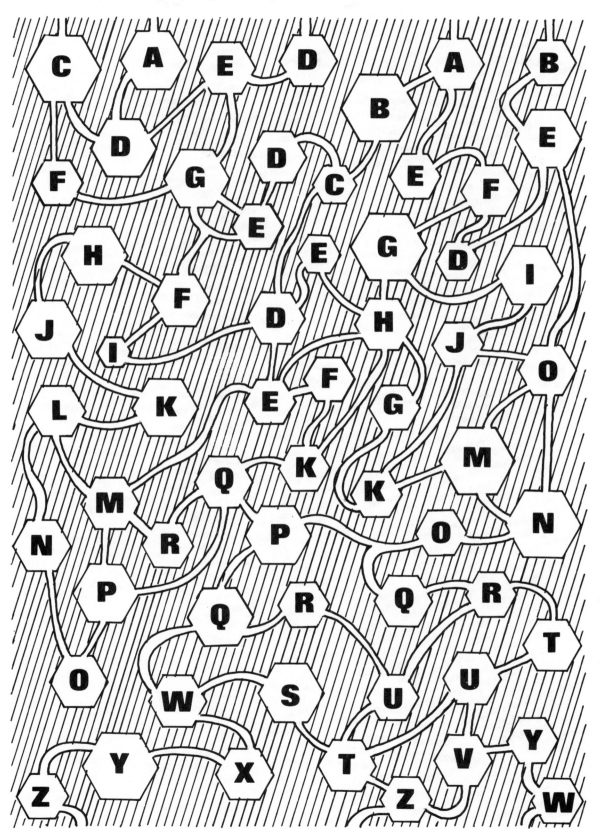

38. ZIG-ADD-ZAG

As you trace your path in this angled maze, you'll do just what the title suggests: zig, add your points, and then zag. If you can end up at the bottom with only fifteen points you're a winnah! Go out there and ZIG!

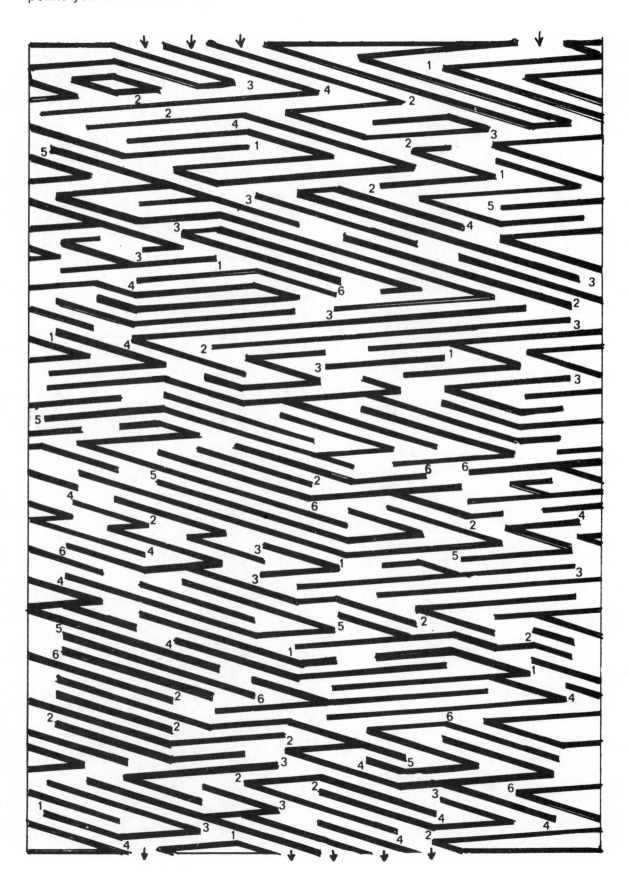

39. A THRU F

Here we present you with the first 6 letters of the alphabet. Start with any one and find out if that one comes out at the bottom. Watch the arrows — no passing one going the wrong direction.

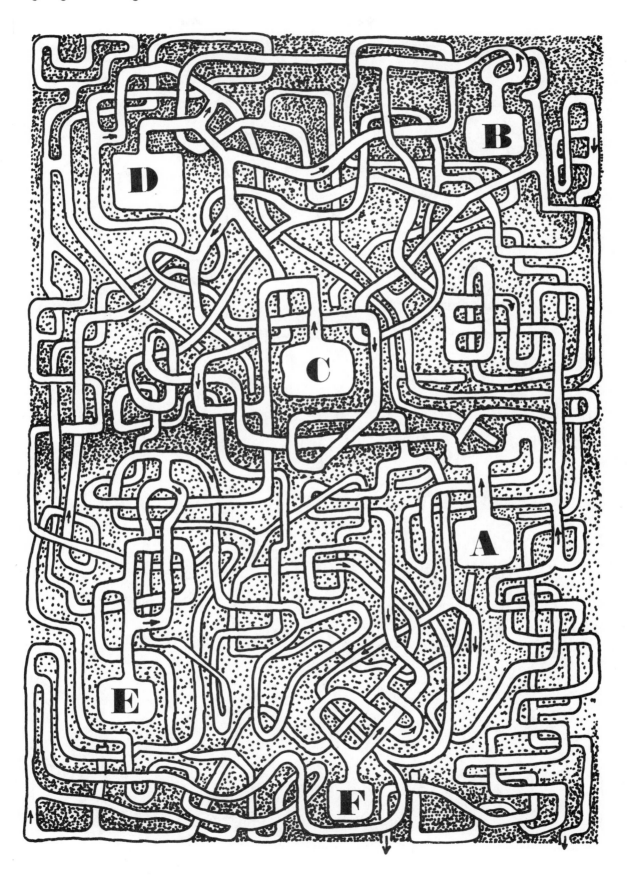

40. BRIDGES & FENCES

Here's a small part of the Thousand Islands. The smart farmers have started charging to go through the gates in their fields — the charge is in dollars as indicated by the number in the opening. You've only got $7, so it's a problem to go from top to bottom.

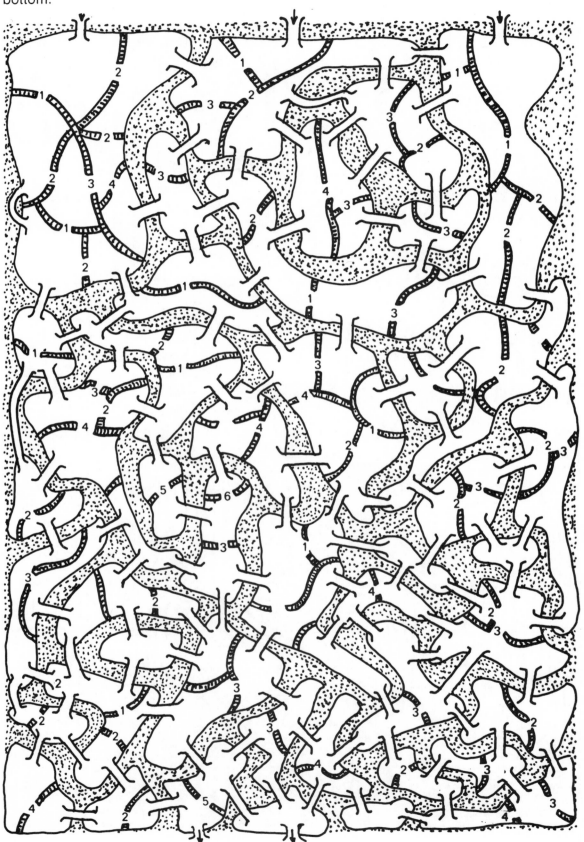

41. KNIGHT'S GAMBIT

If you know chess, this shouldn't be too hard. Your move is that of a Knight, except that instead of moving two squares ahead and one to the right or left, you should move three squares ahead and one to the right or left. The four starting points have dotted lines to give you the idea. YOU MAY ONLY STOP ON AN X-SQUARE. Your move!

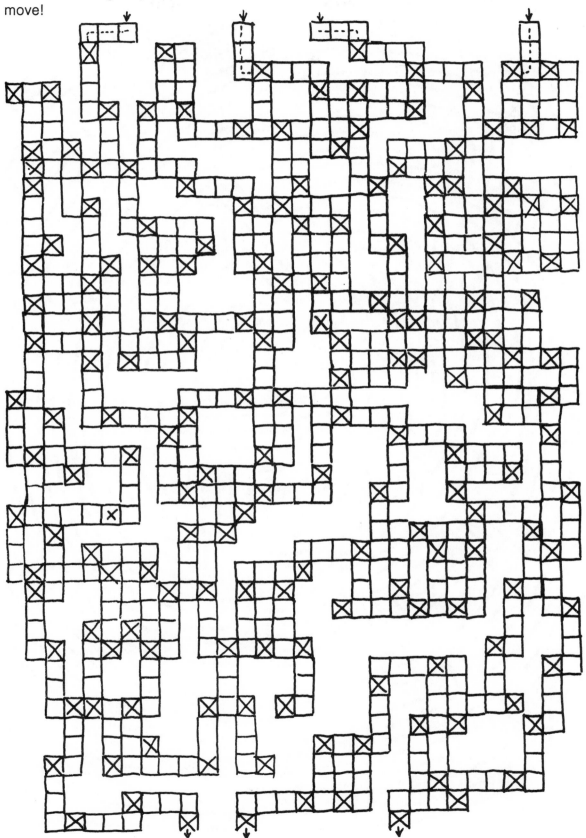

42. CENTER TRIP

READ THESE DIRECTIONS: Many paths go from top to bottom, so the test is to find the one path that passes by the black spot in the center. You must go by that spot to win!

43. NUMBER ROADS

Start at any heavy bordered block at the top. Count off the number of squares indicated — in any direction — and you may come to another numbered block. If you do, count off again. Keep doing so until you land on the X-block at the bottom. You must count out EXACTLY. You may go through a square more than once.

44. ODD MAN OUT

There are lots of ways to travel from top to bottom. However, before you leave you must collect an odd number of points and YOU MAY NOT USE THE SAME PATH TWICE!

45. SOUND OFF

I'm sure it's a relief to tell you that the numbers here have nothing to do with solving this maze. Just go from top to bottom. If you get mad . . . count to ten.

46. PICK A PAIR

Here you have 3 pairs of "islands." Two with a black dot, two with a black square and two with an asterisk. We ask you, as an anthropologist, to start at the top and join one of these pairs. Once you have chosen an island, you must cross it because you cannot use the same path twice. You may not cross any other island to join your pair.

47. QUADRIPUZZLE

Start at the top arrow and when you reach a letter, jump to any similar letter. Starting from this letter, you'll find a third letter and jump again. Finally, one letter's path leads out at the bottom.

48. BRICKYARD

Start from the asterisk at the center. Choose any one of the six paths. Count off the number of squares indicated at the start (don't count the starting square). In almost every case this brings you to another numbered square and you do the same again. Three rules: (1) you must end on any one of the starred squares by an EXACT COUNT; (2) each time you may start in any direction but must continue in that direction for the entire count of that number; (3) don't end your count on an empty square.

1. START OUT

2. VASE & KEY

3. LETTERMIX

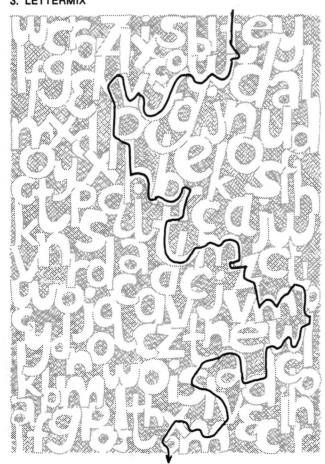

4. PARK RIDE

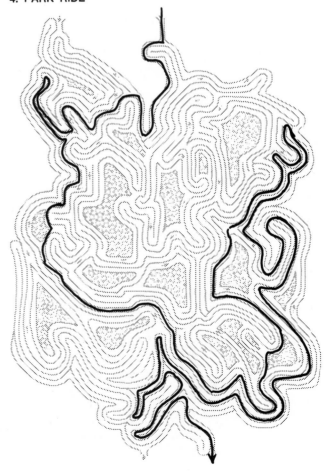

5. K-RATION

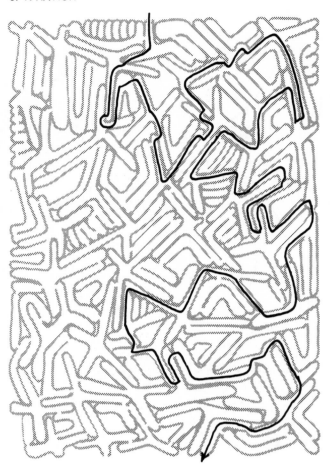

6. DERANGEMENT

7. BONZAI

8. BUBBLE BOUNCE

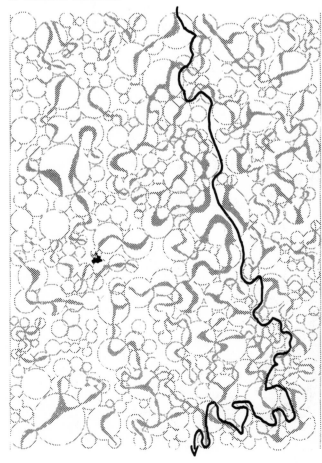

9. TAILSPIN

10. FLORAL DESIGN

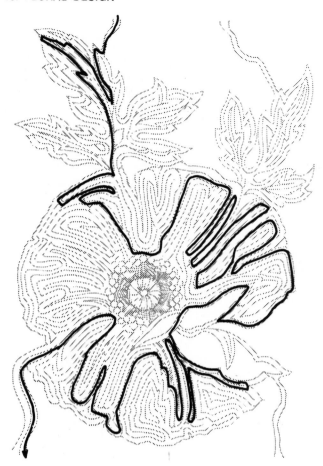

11. CRUMPLES

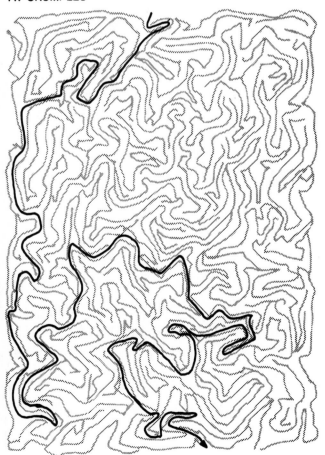

12. NEXI

13. INTERMANGLE

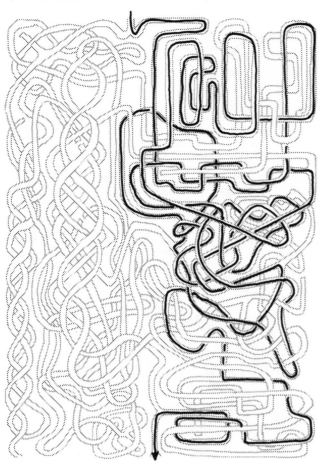

14. HE WENT THATAWAY

15. MASQUE

16. LADYBUGS

17. ALLEY TRAP

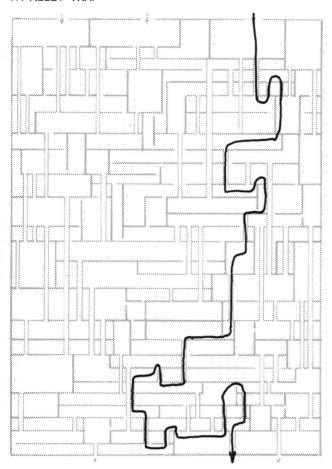

18. BLACK STOPS

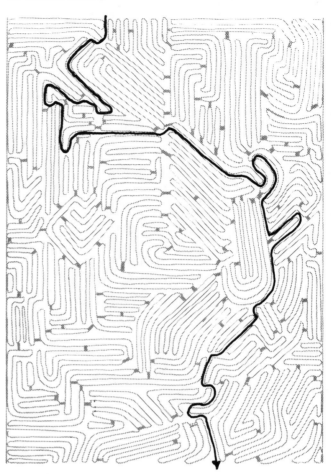

19. CUBE ROUTE

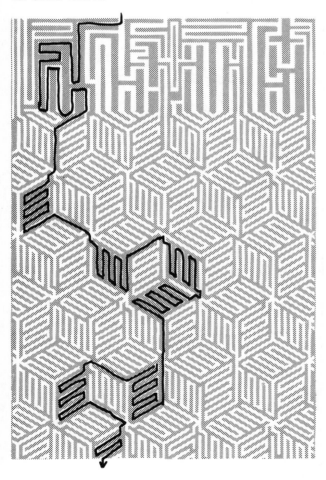

20. TEST PATTERN

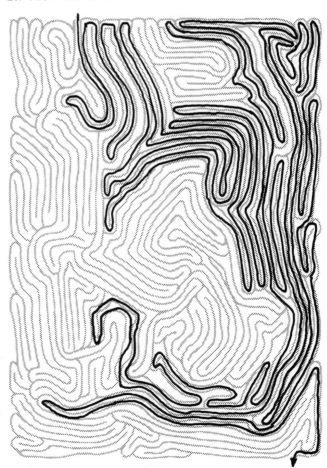

21. QUILTIN' BEE

22. HIGHWAY SIGNS

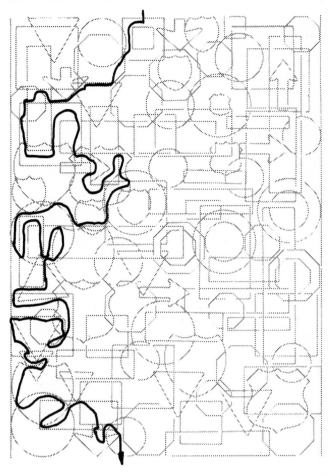

23. BORGIA'S COMPLAINT

24. BOOMERANG

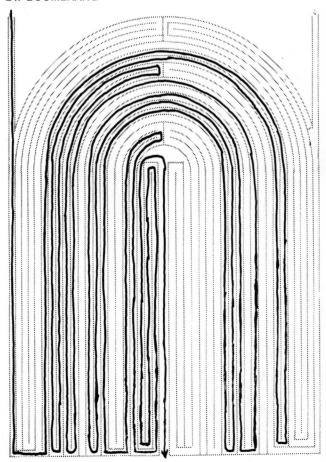

25. FINE FOURTH

26. PINBALL

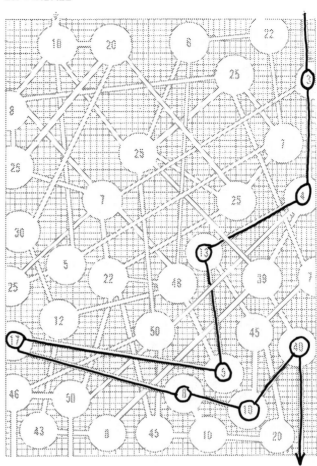

27. OUTBOUND

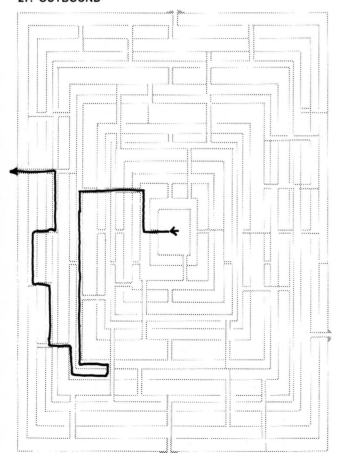

28. WILLIAM TELLS

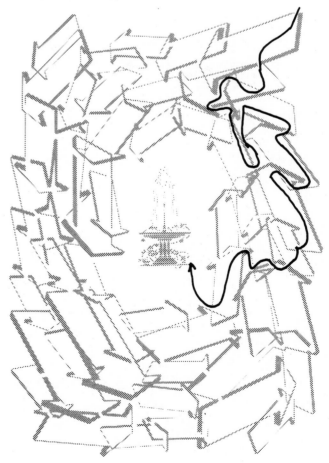

29. LETTER JUMP

30. MONKEY SEE . . .

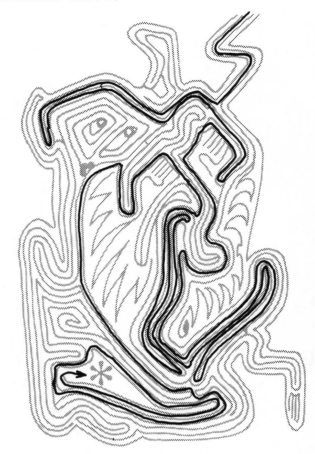

31. TANGLED WEB

32. NO! NO!

33. ANGLES & CURVES

34. EVEN MONEY

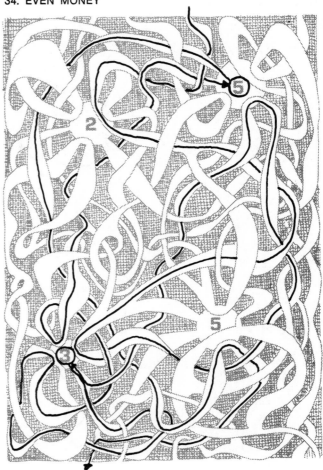

35. BOLD LINES

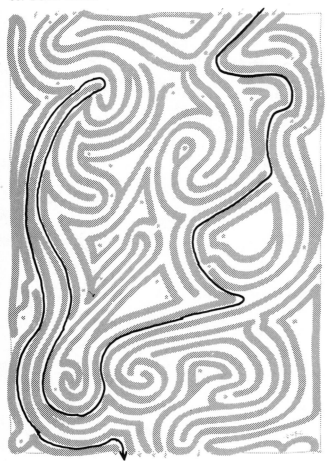

36. MIXMAZE

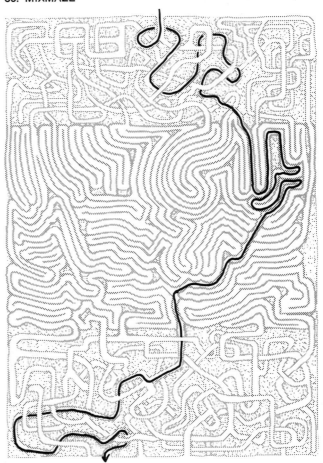

37. ETAOIN SHRDLU

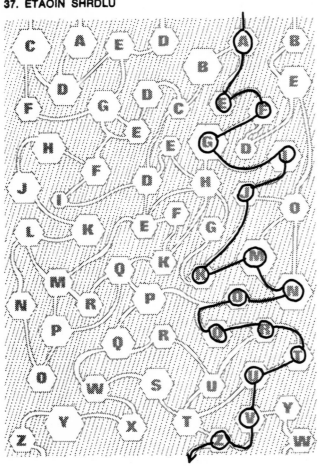

38. ZIG-ADD-ZAG

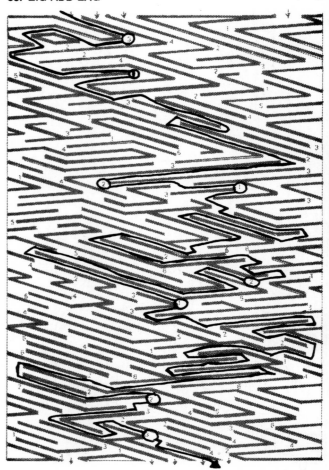

39. A THRU F

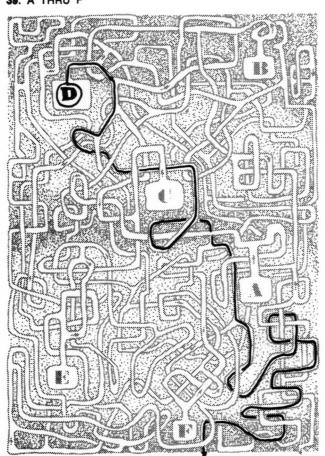

40. BRIDGES & FENCES

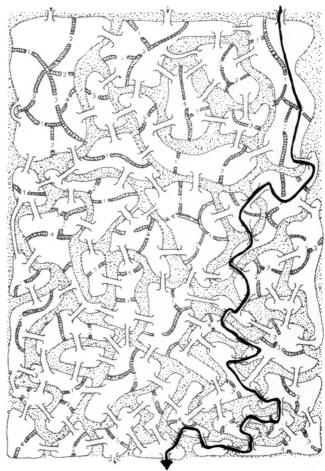

41. KNIGHT'S GAMBIT

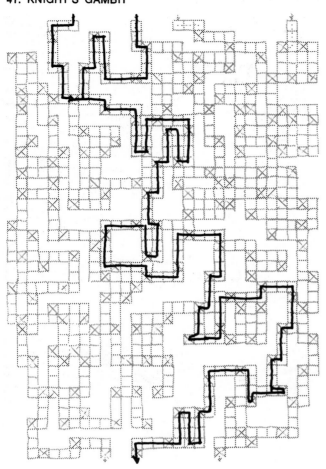

42. CENTER TRIP

43. NUMBER ROADS

44. ODD MAN OUT

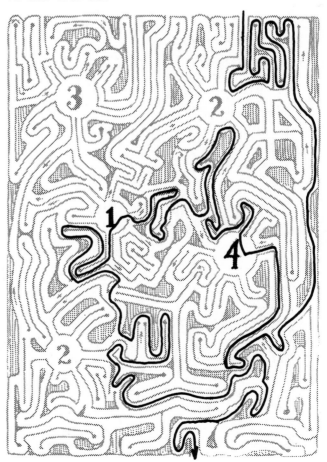

45. SOUND OFF

46. PICK A PAIR

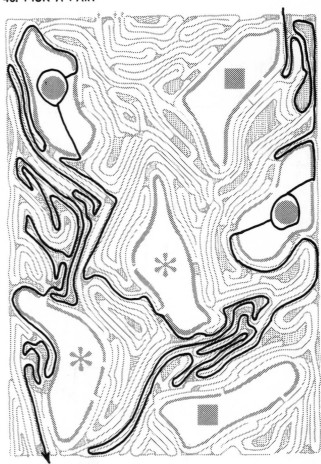

47. QUADRIPUZZLE

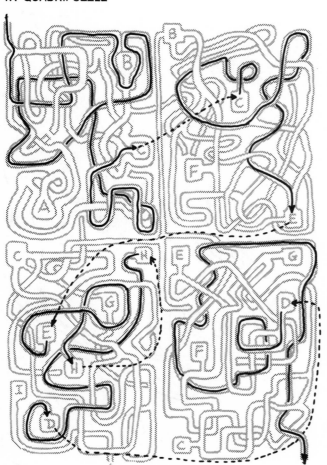

48. BRICKYARD